THE CLIMATE CRISIS IN THE WEST

by Susan B. Katz

FOCUS READERS®
NAVIGATOR

WWW.FOCUSREADERS.COM

Copyright © 2024 by Focus Readers®, Lake Elmo, MN 55042. All rights reserved. No part of this book may be reproduced or utilized in any form or by any means without written permission from the publisher.

Focus Readers is distributed by North Star Editions:
sales@northstareditions.com | 888-417-0195

Produced for Focus Readers by Red Line Editorial.

Content Consultant: Tim Brown, PhD, Research Professor of Climatology, Desert Research Institute

Photographs ©: iStockphoto, cover, 1; Noah Berger/AP Images, 4–5; Renée C. Byer/ZumaPress/Newscom, 7; Shutterstock Images, 8–9, 13, 16–17, 19, 22–23, 25; Red Line Editorial, 11; David Goldman/AP Images, 15; Nic Coury/AP Images, 21; Cecilio Ricardo/USDA Forest Service, 27; Carlos Avila Gonzalez/San Francisco Chronicle/AP Images, 29

Library of Congress Cataloging-in-Publication Data
Library of Congress Cataloging-in-Publication Data is available on the Library of Congress website.

ISBN
978-1-63739-638-4 (hardcover)
978-1-63739-695-7 (paperback)
978-1-63739-803-6 (ebook pdf)
978-1-63739-752-7 (hosted ebook)

Printed in the United States of America
Mankato, MN
082023

ABOUT THE AUTHOR
Susan B. Katz is a National Board Certified Teacher and bilingual educator with more than 30 years of classroom expertise. She is the author of more than 50 children's books, including more than a dozen STEAM titles. Susan studied environmental science at the University of Michigan, School of Natural Resources and the Environment, and worked in a Costa Rican rainforest.

TABLE OF CONTENTS

CHAPTER 1
The Mosquito Fire 5

CHAPTER 2
The Climate of the West 9

THAT'S AMAZING!
Frank Kanawha Lake 14

CHAPTER 3
Crises in the West 17

CHAPTER 4
Many Solutions 23

Focus on the West • 30
Glossary • 31
To Learn More • 32
Index • 32

CHAPTER 1

THE MOSQUITO FIRE

In September 2022, the California hills lit up. Flames from the Mosquito Fire were fast approaching. Janet Stickler had to leave her home in Northern California. After driving an hour north, she found a place to stay. But a week later, Stickler had to leave again. Another wildfire had started nearby.

The Mosquito Fire burns in Northern California.

Meanwhile, the Mosquito Fire kept burning. Thousands of people had to leave their homes. Nearly 100 buildings were destroyed or damaged. The fire burned more than 70,000 acres (28,000 hectares) of land. It was California's largest wildfire in 2022.

More than 1,000 firefighters worked to put out the fire. After a few weeks, the fire was mostly under control. People returned home. No one was hurt.

Even so, the experience was difficult. One class helped its students deal with what had happened. They shared how it felt to leave home. Then the class worked together to write a song. Writing the song

A girl looks for toys at a center for people who left their homes because of the Mosquito Fire.

helped the class process their feelings from the fire.

Wildfires are becoming more common across the West. Scientists have linked **climate change** to worsening wildfires. As a result, more and more people are facing this form of extreme event.

CHAPTER 2

THE CLIMATE OF THE WEST

Weather and climate both involve what happens in an area's atmosphere. They describe temperature and **precipitation**. They describe wind, sunshine, and **humidity**, too. Weather is about these conditions at a specific time and place. In contrast, climate describes an area's long-term weather patterns.

California's Pacific coast stretches for hundreds of miles.

The West has a variety of climates. The California coast tends to be mild. That's due to the Pacific Ocean. Ocean water heats up and cools down more slowly than land does. As a result, the coast does not often get very hot or cold.

Instead, coastal areas have just two seasons. They are the rainy and dry seasons. May to October tends to be dry. November to April is wetter.

Inland, the region's climate is different. Mountain ranges, including the Sierra Nevada, run north to south. High in the mountains, temperatures drop. In winter, these areas can receive plenty of snow. But droughts also happen in winter. They lower the amount of snow available for rivers, streams, lakes, and groundwater.

The West's mountains often block moisture from the Pacific Ocean. For this reason, areas east of the mountains are dry. They have **arid** and desert

THE WEST

landscapes. In fact, Nevada is the driest US state.

The West depends on the mountains for much of its fresh water. During the winter, snow falls and piles up, forming a snowpack. In the spring, melting snowpack flows down the mountains.

THE COAST MIWOK

Coast Miwok peoples live in Northern California. These **Indigenous** groups have lived there for thousands of years. Traditionally, the Coast Miwok used fire to manage the environment. They harvested seeds and plants in the fall. Then they set controlled fires in the grasslands. The fires released the dead plants' nutrients into the soil. The nutrients helped the plants grow back the next year.

Death Valley in California is one of the hottest places on Earth.

This water enters rivers. Then some water flows into **reservoirs**.

For example, Lake Mead is in southern Nevada. The reservoir takes in water from the Colorado River. Lake Mead supplies water to Southern Nevada and Southern California. It also sends water to many farms. These farms provide food for much of the United States.

THAT'S AMAZING!

FRANK KANAWHA LAKE

For many Indigenous peoples, living with fire was a way of life. The Karuk and Yurok are Indigenous peoples of Northern California. For thousands of years, the Karuk and Yurok set controlled burns. These fires burn extra-dry parts of a forest. That helps prevent forest fires from getting out of control. As a result, berries and nuts continue to grow in good supply.

In the early 1900s, the US government ended these practices. But that started to change in the 1990s. Today, many people are working to bring back these methods. One person is Frank Kanawha Lake. Lake is a forest scientist. He is Karuk with Yurok family.

A member of the Yurok Tribe takes part in a training for controlled burns in 2021.

In 1994, Lake joined the US Forest Service. He has helped educate the US government. Lake has shown how traditional burns help prevent serious wildfires.

CHAPTER 3

CRISES IN THE WEST

Humans are the main cause of climate change. Using **fossil fuels** is the major reason. Burning these fuels releases **greenhouse gases** into the atmosphere. These gases are raising Earth's average temperature.

This temperature increase is happening across California and Nevada. Extremely

Between 1970 and 2020, Las Vegas, Nevada, became nearly 5.76 degrees Fahrenheit (3.2°C) hotter. That was the most of any US city.

hot days are becoming more common. This heat can be especially harmful in cities. Urban areas contain little natural land. Instead, they are covered with buildings and pavement. These surfaces absorb heat. Then they release that heat back into the air. That makes hot days and

LAKE MEAD

Nevada has long been a desert. But climate change is making the state even drier. There has been extreme heat and less snowmelt across the West. These events have taken a toll. Lakes are drying up. In 2022, Lake Mead was only 27 percent full. Officials declared a megadrought. That is a drought lasting for decades.

Low water levels are clearly visible at Lake Mead. The white rock was last covered in 2000.

nights even hotter. This process is called the urban heat island effect.

Higher temperatures also make droughts worse. Heat causes more water to **evaporate**. Plants and soil hold on to less moisture. Plus, climate change is making drought more common.

A drought happens when there is less rain and snow. In winter, that means there is less snowpack. Then, less water flows into reservoirs. As a result, water supplies run low.

Together, hot and dry conditions cause other problems. One major threat is wildfire. Drier forests catch fire much more easily. These conditions also make wildfire season last longer.

Every year, wildfires force thousands of people in the West to leave their homes. People lose their homes. Animal habitats are destroyed, too. Plus, wildfire smoke travels far beyond the fire. The smoke makes the air unsafe to breathe.

Western wildfires are occurring more often throughout the year. They used to take place more seasonally.

Wildfires can also lead to other disasters. Severe fires kill much of an area's plants. These plants help absorb rainwater. Without them, floods are more likely after heavy rains. Plants also help keep the ground more stable. In hilly areas, fewer plants can lead to more mudslides.

CHAPTER 4

MANY SOLUTIONS

People across the West are working to slow climate change. The most important way is reducing fossil fuel use. For example, California took a big step in 2022. The governor announced the state would shift away from gasoline-powered cars. California would stop selling new gasoline cars by 2035.

In 2020, transportation was the largest single source of greenhouse gas emissions in the United States.

Transportation is a major cause of climate change. And California is an important state. It has the highest population of any US state. It also has the world's fifth-largest economy. As a result, California's decisions often impact other parts of the country. Car experts said California's decision could speed up a nationwide shift to electric cars. These vehicles run on electricity instead of gasoline. As a result, switching to electric vehicles can decrease the use of fossil fuels.

Even so, the climate crisis is already here. So, California and Nevada must also adapt to climate change. During droughts,

Growing hay for cattle uses massive amounts of water in the West.

managing water use is key. Individuals can help save water. For instance, people can water their lawns less often.

However, farming uses most of the water in the West. Farming and water experts argue for larger changes. They say farms should grow less corn, rice, and hay. These crops use lots of water.

25

Instead, farms could shift to plants such as beans. Beans need much less water to grow.

In addition, laws about using water led to problems. In 2022, the main water laws were more than 100 years old. They were passed long before climate change. As a result, the laws did not promote saving water. Water experts argue that new laws are needed.

Wildfires are another area of focus. Wildfire experts say the region can manage forests better. Workers can use controlled burns. These fires remove dead plants and trees. People can also thin forests. This gets rid of dead or

In 2021, workers helped thin forests across the West, including California's Lassen National Forest.

unhealthy trees. Both methods reduce flammable materials. That makes it harder for wildfires to spread.

Cities can adapt to dangerous heat waves. Buildings can be constructed with more insulation. They also can use cooling systems that save more energy. In addition, cities can increase green space. Parks and trees provide shade for people and buildings.

Many cities are taking other steps. For instance, Los Angeles, California, tried something new in 2022. The city hired its first-ever Chief Heat Officer. The officer

RESTORING MÁYALA WÁTA

Máyala Wáta is a meadow near Lake Tahoe. This lake is on the California-Nevada border. Washoe people had managed the area for thousands of years. But in the 1800s, US settlers drove the Washoe out of the area. They also destroyed the ecosystem there. However, in 2020, the Washoe Tribe began restoring the meadow. This project aimed to reduce wildfire risk. It also aimed to help the area deal with drought.

Buildings can have plants or even gardens on their roofs. This greenery can help keep buildings cooler.

aimed to educate people about the city's cooling centers. She also worked on making a new map of the city. The map will help show what areas are most vulnerable to extreme heat.

Across the West, people are feeling the effects of climate change. The problems are serious. But many groups are working to help the region through the crisis.

FOCUS ON
THE WEST

Write your answers on a separate piece of paper.

1. Write a letter to an adult explaining what people in the West can do to adapt to climate change.

2. Do you think it's important to cut down on water usage at home even if your community isn't experiencing a drought? Why or why not?

3. Lake Mead gathers water from what body of water?

    A. Pacific Ocean
    B. Colorado River
    C. Lake Tahoe

4. Why can extreme heat be worse in cities?

    A. Cities' buildings and pavement absorb heat.
    B. Cities' natural areas can catch fire easily.
    C. Cities tend to be near large bodies of water.

Answer key on page 32.

GLOSSARY

arid
Very dry as a result of getting little rain.

climate change
A human-caused global crisis involving long-term changes in Earth's temperature and weather patterns.

evaporate
To change from a liquid to a gas.

fossil fuels
Energy sources that come from the remains of plants and animals that died long ago.

greenhouse gases
Gases that trap heat in Earth's atmosphere.

humidity
The amount of moisture in the air.

Indigenous
Native to a region, or belonging to ancestors who lived in a region before colonists arrived.

precipitation
Water that falls from clouds to the ground. It can be in the form of rain, hail, or snow.

reservoirs
Human-made lakes used for water supply storage.

TO LEARN MORE

BOOKS

Henzel, Cynthia Kennedy. *Redesigning Cities to Fight Climate Change*. Lake Elmo, MN: Focus Readers, 2023.

Huddleston, Emma. *Adapting to Climate Change*. Minneapolis: Abdo Publishing, 2021.

Raij, Emily. *Climate Change and You: How Climate Change Affects Your Life*. North Mankato, MN: Capstone Press, 2020.

NOTE TO EDUCATORS

Visit **www.focusreaders.com** to find lesson plans, activities, links, and other resources related to this title.

INDEX

California, 5–6, 10–13, 14, 17, 23–24, 28
Coast Miwok, 12
Colorado River, 11, 13

droughts, 10–11, 18–20, 24, 28

farms, 13, 25–26

Karuk, 14

Lake, Frank Kanawha, 14–15
Lake Mead, 11, 13, 18
Los Angeles, California, 11, 28–29

Máyala Wáta, 28
Mosquito Fire, 5–7

Nevada, 11–13, 17–18, 24, 28

Pacific Ocean, 10–11

Sierra Nevada, 10–11

Washoe Tribe, 28
wildfires, 5–7, 15, 20–21, 26–28

Yurok, 14

Answer Key: 1. Answers will vary; **2.** Answers will vary; **3.** B; **4.** A